# CHERRY CHENG'S
## WRITING JOURNAL
(How-to-write stuff for English)

**NOT SUITABLE FOR TEACHERS**

Published by Era Publications,
220 Grange Road, Flinders Park, SA 5025 Australia

*Cherry Cheng's Writing Journal*
Copyright © June Loves 2001
Printed in Hong Kong
First published 2001

Illustrated and designed by Lisa James

All rights reserved by the publisher

*National Library of Australia Cataloguing-in-Publication data*:

Loves, June, 1938-.
Cherry Cheng's writing journal (how to write stuff for English)

Includes index

ISBN 1 86374 604 8

1. English language - Writing - Study and teaching (Primary). 2. English language - Composition and exercises - Study and teaching (Primary). I. Title

372.623044

For worldwide distribution details of this publication see Era Publications' web site
**www.erapublications.com**

15   14   13   12   11   10   9   8   7   6   5   4   3   2   1

# Contents

| | |
|---|---|
| How to use this book | 4 |
| List of characters | 5 |
| **Trapped for two nights and three days!** | 6 |
| **Murder in room 548!** | 8 |
| *How to write a murder mystery* | 10 |
| **Anton's broken heart** | 12 |
| *How to write an explanation* | 14 |
| **A mouse hunt!** | 17 |
| *How to write an advertisement* | 21 |
| *How to write a report* | 22 |
| **Trouble again!** | 25 |
| *How to write a recount* | 26 |
| **A free fringe trim!** | 28 |
| *How to write a narrative* | 30 |
| **The Carlo interview** | 34 |
| *How to write news reports from interviews* | 36 |
| *How to write a procedural text* | 38 |
| *How to write an email* | 40 |
| **Fine dining!** | 42 |
| **A life-threatening dilemma** | 43 |
| *How to write poetry* | 46 |
| *How to write notices, messages and memos* | 48 |
| **Hotel wildlife!** | 50 |
| **The wedding** | 51 |
| *Extra poetry* | 54 |
| *How to write a newspaper recount* | 56 |
| Quick reference | 58 |
|     Glossary | 58 |
|     Index | 62 |

Dedication:
A heartfelt thank you to Brianna and Hayley for all their help. J.L.

# How to use this book

This book contains the journal entries I wrote when I was stuck in a four-star hotel for two nights and three days. My journal includes useful how-to-write stuff for English.

You can:
- read this book from beginning to end;
- just read my journal entries, and skip the 'how-to-write stuff for English' until later;
- skip my journal entries — although they're a very exciting read — and just read the 'how-to-write stuff';
- use my writing samples as models when you have to do an English assignment.

Good luck with your writing!
Cherry Cheng

*P.S. If you're really desperate and have to do a writing assignment immediately, use the 'Quick reference' section at the back of my book. Check the glossary and index.*

**Acknowledgments**
My mother Angela Cheng and my grandmother Lily Cheng
The English Teachers' Association, particularly Imogen Brunetti (secretary of the Association) for permission to take bits from the English Teachers' Association handouts (about how to teach different kinds of writing)
The staff at the Grand Hotel
Tammy Bjork, my best friend, for permission to print her poems 'Eternity' and 'The Mouse'

# List of characters

Characters in a book can be people, animals or things. Below is a list of the characters who appear in my writing guide. Some surnames have been left out to protect privacy. You have to be careful when you use true-life characters in your book. They could sue you!

Cherry

*My family, friends and acquaintances*
**Tammy Bjork** — my best friend.
**Imogen Brunetti** — secretary of the English Teachers' Association and my mother's best friend
**Angela Cheng** — my mother
**Cherry Cheng** — me (the writer)
**Lily Cheng** — my grandmother from my dad's side of the family (and owner of The Golden Dragon restaurant)
**Grant McKenna** — my good friend who happens to be a boy. He doesn't star in this book
**Mr Sinclair and Ms Honeywell** — My science and English teachers, who do not star in this book but are mentioned

*Hotel staff and guests*
**Alma** — room attendant
**Mabel Brown** — housekeeper at the Grand Hotel where Mum and I stayed. Mabel has six kids, but they don't come into this book.
**Fred Brown** — Mabel's husband (he doesn't work at the Grand Hotel)
**George** — the houseman
**Harry** — hotel handyman (who works in the maintenance department) at the Grand Hotel
**Henry** — hotel valet
**Gloria** — conference facilitator at the Grand Hotel
**James** — concierge at the Grand Hotel
**Jess** — florist at Park Flowers, another shop in the Grand Hotel
**Joeline and Shane** — in-house gym instructors in the rooftop gym and sauna at the Grand Hotel
**Anton Le Fevre** — handsome young waiter at the Grand Hotel
**Helen Papadopolous** — beautiful young cook at the Grand Hotel
**Mr and Mrs Papadopolous** — Helen Papadopolous's parents
**Winston Pickles** — guest relations manager at the Grand Hotel
**Joe Rickard** — manager of the Park Cafe and piano player in the Park Lounge. The Park Cafe and the Park Lounge are part of the Grand Hotel.
**Simon and Rachel** — hotel guests
**Trish** — hairdresser at the Park Hair Salon, one of the shops in the Grand Hotel
**Carlo Tarantino** — executive chef at the Grand Hotel

# Trapped for two nights and three days!
Friday 9.00 am

I wrote this journal because I was trapped. Trapped in a luxury four-star hotel for two nights and three days! Actually I wasn't *exactly* trapped — I just had to be there. And keep out of trouble!

My mother was on a three-day conference for English teachers. (She teaches English, but not at my school thank heaven!)

As well as working in The Golden Dragon with Grandma, my mum studied for years to be an English teacher. For the last year I thought Mum was studying a famous person called John Rah. But she wasn't; she'd been studying genre! *Genre* is pronounced *jon-rah*. It just means different kinds of writing. If your English teacher is like mine, Ms Honeywell, and Mum they just love students to do lots of different kinds of writing — narratives, recounts, poetry, letters, descriptions etc.

The English Teachers' Conference was about teaching kids how to write different kinds of stuff. It was held in a huge hotel for the first three days of the summer break.

Mum couldn't get anyone to look after me so I had to go too.

Grandma Cheng was going to look after me, but the cook at her restaurant, The Golden Dragon, broke his arm practising for a dragon boat race, so Grandma had to be cook again.

After Grandpa died, Grandma Cheng kept working full-time in The Golden Dragon. Now that she's retired, she just keeps an eye on the restaurant.

Grandma Cheng was really upset that she couldn't look after me. I said I would be fine on my own while she worked at the restaurant. But no way would Mum or Grandma Cheng hear of that! Anyway, Grandma Cheng offered to pay for me to stay at the Grand Hotel with Mum for the two nights and three days. And *if* I could keep out of trouble she would buy me a pair of state-of-the-art in-line skates and trendy skate gear.

Mum was desperate. She said yes immediately!

Basically I do not believe in bribery. However, my two best friends, Tammy and Grant, both have in-line skates. Tammy shares her blades with me, but Grant's are too big. It would be really cool if I had my own.

Grandma Cheng said to look on the state-of-the-art in-line skates and trendy gear as a reward for keeping out of trouble.

I said yes too!

We packed our car with camping gear. After three days in the hotel, we were heading up the coast for a camping holiday.

I started to concentrate on keeping out of trouble. Not that I go after trouble — it's more like trouble comes after me.

The Grand Hotel was gorgeous. Masses of pink marble and oak panelling, elegant gold dangling lights and super ceilings.

I can absolutely recommend it to anyone who wants a luxurious three-day stay.

We checked in at the reception desk and Mum dashed off to her first session of the teachers' conference. I promised faithfully, cross my heart and hope to die, to keep out of trouble until I met her in the lobby for lunch at 1.30 pm.

Our room was number 541; 5 stands for the fifth floor, 41 is the number of the room. It had a balcony overlooking the Palm Courtyard with breathtaking views of the city — if you jumped up and down.

Our room was exactly as described in the hotel brochure: brilliantly appointed.

It had a marble bathroom, two beds, a couch, deep-pile carpet, TV, tea and coffee-making facilities, a fridge (stacked with snacks and drinks which I wasn't allowed to touch — except for the ice — because they go on your bill), telephone, coffee table, tasteful curtains, bedspreads and framed prints.

There was even a bowl of fruit and some magazines.

Hugo, the porter, delivered our bags. (I explained that Mum hadn't left me any money to tip him. He said, 'No worries!' because he had just collected a huge tip from a basketball team on the tenth floor.)

After I unpacked our bags, I checked the Hotel Directory and set out to explore the hotel.

I had only walked ten paces when I heard a bloodcurdling scream.

The scream spelt trouble — *trouble* with a capital T!

## Murder in room 548!
### Friday 9.30 am

'Murder! Murder!'

The cries were coming from Room 548. The door burst open.

A woman stumbled out! She looked awful; her face was white as a ghost. Blood was on one of her white shoes, and on the hem of her uniform.

The woman grabbed hold of me.

'Help me!' she cried.

'Sure,' I said. I helped her to sit on the carpet in the hall, with her back against the wall. 'What's your name?' I asked.

'Mabel,' she gasped. 'I'm the housekeeper on the fifth floor.'

Mabel looked as if she was going to faint. I told her to put her head between her legs while I stuck my head in room 548.

No one there. Nothing out of place!

'Where's the murder victim Mabel?'

'In the bathroom,' she gasped. 'I'll show you.'

We crept into room 548. I opened the bathroom door very slowly.

There on the floor, was a very squashed, very bloody, very dead mouse!

'Is this the victim?' I asked.

'Yes,' Mabel said weakly. 'The poor little creature. I've killed it. I didn't mean to. It was under my foot. I feel so awful! How could I have murdered such a little creature?'

She began to cry.

'Don't cry,' I said, as I scraped the mouse from the floor, stuffed it into the waste bin, then washed the mouse blood from my hands.

'Is there anywhere we can get a cup of tea?'

Grandma Cheng believes tea can solve most problems.

'We can go to the staffroom,' Mabel said, wiping the blood from her shoe. 'It's on this floor.'

I helped Mabel stack her trolley with her cleaning gear. We parked it outside the staffroom and went inside for a calming cup of tea.

The mouse mystery was very puzzling. How could one little mouse get into the bathroom of room 548? The Grand Hotel seemed a very clean, mouse-free hotel to me.

(Story continues on page 12.)

# How to write a murder mystery

Murder mysteries are also called crime fiction, whodunits and detective or suspense fiction.

Before you begin to write your story, make a plan. Start with the ending! Answer these questions:
- Who was murdered?
- Who was the murderer?

The main character in a murder mystery or crime fiction is a detective, sleuth or private eye. Apart from the person who committed the murder, and the murder victim, you will need other mysterious or suspicious characters in your story to confuse the reader.

## *Why?*
Work out a reason for the murder. Was it greed, revenge or power?

## *Where?*
Where did the murder take place? You need a setting — like a staffroom, a hotel or a creepy old mansion.

If you are writing about a particular time in history, you will need to research how people lived, what they wore, what they ate or how they travelled. You can't say *Ralph hopped into his gleaming red sports car. He finished eating his packet of crisps. Nonchalantly he screwed up the empty packet and tossed it onto the concrete driveway* if cars, packets of crisps and concrete hadn't been invented at the time of your story.

## *When?*
When did the murder happen? Work out carefully when things happened. Some readers are really smart and can pick up mistakes in your writing.

## *Create atmosphere*
A murder mystery should have a spooky, eerie atmosphere, eg *The house was filled with the whispering voices of long dead relatives.*

## *Plant clues and red herrings (false clues)*
If a knife is a clue in the murder, write about it early in your story, eg *The knife glinted in the sunlight as it rested on the kitchen bench.* Red herrings are false clues, eg *The maid had blood all over her apron.* This might be a red herring, because the blood on the maid's apron came from her cut finger, not the murder victim.

## A FRAMEWORK FOR WRITING MURDER MYSTERIES

**Beginning**

Introduce the:

- victim
- person who finds the body
- scene of the crime
- detective, sleuth or private eye

**Middle**

Introduce the:

- suspects (about five to ten characters), and have the detective, sleuth or private eye interview or investigate them
- clues and red herrings (false clues)
- any sub-plots (love, jealousy, greed etc)

**End**

- Eliminate suspects as you zero in on the criminal.
- Confront and arrest the criminal.
- Explain clues. All red herrings (false clues) must be revealed too.
- Stop the suspense.

## *Handy hints for writing murder mysteries*

When you write a murder mystery, the plot should get thicker and thicker. This means you introduce more clues and suspects. The reader should still be guessing at what really happened until about the last chapter, or even the last page.

Grandma Cheng loves reading murder mysteries — she calls them 'whodunits'. She advises writers not to leave the solution to the last page, because the reader can get annoyed if the last page of the book is damaged or missing. It's like being sent to bed before you've seen the end of a terrific TV program, and no one else at school has seen it either.

## Anton's broken heart
### Friday 11.00 am

In the staffroom everyone was super-friendly. I told them that Mabel was upset because she murdered a mouse in room 548. Mabel's fellow workers were very supportive.

Then I met Anton, who is French and drop-dead gorgeous! He's the head waiter in the hotel's Park Dining Room.

Anton says Mabel is a good friend. Mabel and her family took Anton under their wing when he started working at the hotel. He stayed at their house until he found a flat of his own. Anton and Fred, Mabel's husband, go fishing together, and Mabel's kids (she's got six) just adore Anton.

Anton was getting support from his fellow workers too, because he was suffering from a broken heart. Helen, a chef in the Park Restaurant, is the love of Anton's life. Helen broke off their engagement last week. This was a tragedy.

Anton and Helen were supposed to be married in the Palm Courtyard on Sunday night. The hotel management were letting Anton hire the Palm Courtyard at a cheap rate because he is a staff member. You could see the Palm Courtyard from our balcony; I knew it would be a stunning place for a wedding. It's an open part of the hotel where you can sit, and eat or drink. It has a spectacular waterfall, a fountain, a fishpond with water lilies, and of course, loads of tropical palms.

Anton was devastated — he said his heart was breaking into a thousand little pieces.

Anton and Helen met when Helen was backpacking through Europe. They fell head-over-heels when they worked together in a cafe in Paris. Anton said he took one look into Helen's dark brown eyes and was instantly in love.

Helen returned to Australia and Anton followed her about a month later. He got a job working in the hotel to be near Helen, and one starlit evening, he proposed to her in the Palm Courtyard.

Helen immediately said yes. However, obstacles were strewn along their path of love. Helen's family is Greek, and they wanted her to marry a wealthy Greek boy so they didn't agree with her plans to marry Anton. (Anton's family didn't mind, I guess because they were miles away in France.)

In spite of the opposition from Helen's family, Anton and Helen decided to go ahead with their wedding plans for this Sunday. Anton has been saving for the wedding. (Helen saved for her dress. They were both saving for a down payment on a restaurant.)

Then tragedy struck — Helen's family kicked up such a fuss that Helen called the wedding off. For good!

Anton is heartbroken and in the deepest, darkest despair. I can understand this.

I told Anton he shouldn't give up. It was only Friday. He still had two days to talk Helen into getting married. The sad thing is, if Helen does decide to marry Anton, her family will never talk to her again.

Mabel and the other staff members thought it was a really tragic situation. Mabel said Helen has already bought her wedding dress and Anton will lose his deposit on the Palm Courtyard for the reception.

Altogether, it would be an awful waste if they didn't get married on Sunday.

(Story continues on page 17.)

# How to write an explanation

An explanation text is writing that explains how something works or why it works. The sample below is my explanation text 'How the heart works'. Anton says his heart is breaking, but a heart doesn't have anything to do with feelings of love or sadness — that's the brain! However, our heart is important in keeping us alive because it keeps blood moving around our body.

## How the heart works

*heading and opening statement to describe topic*

The heart is a pump that keeps blood moving around the body twenty-four hours a day. It is a bag of strong muscle. The heart pushes blood around the body by contracting and then relaxing to let the blood flow through.

*events written in a logical sequence to explain process – how and why*

The heart is divided into four parts — two parts on each side. There is a left and right atrium above a left and right ventricle. The two sides of the heart work independently. On the left side, fresh blood carrying oxygen from the lungs enters the left atrium. Then blood is forced through a valve down to the left ventricle.

*linking to show cause and effect*

The valve closes after the blood has gone through, so the blood does not flow backwards.

*use of present tense*

The oxygen-rich blood is forced into the body's main artery, the aorta, and then out of the heart ready to flow around the body. On the right side, stale blood carrying waste such as carbon dioxide enters the right atrium and passes into the right ventricle. Then it is pumped out to the lungs where it leaves carbon dioxide and picks up oxygen.

P.S. Always read through your work to make sure you understand your explanation!

# A FRAMEWORK FOR WRITING EXPLANATIONS

You may need to research your topic to find out facts, and information that explains the facts.

**Introduction**
Begin by telling the reader what you are talking about (often a heading, a statement or a question).

**Detailed explanation**
Follow with a logical sequence of events.
- Use words like *first, following, then, after* and *finally* to explain things in order.
- Use mainly present tense verbs like *is, are, happens, works*.
- Use words like *if/then, so, consequently* and *because* to link cause and effect in sentences. Try to avoid unnecessary words.

# How to
## Handy hints for writing explanations

- You can use diagrams, illustrations, graphs or charts to add to your written explanations. An explanatory diagram may be just one drawing, or a series of drawings.
- You can use close-ups (enlargements) to focus on important features.
- Labels can be used to locate parts of a diagram, with a line or arrow to connect the word or information to the diagram.

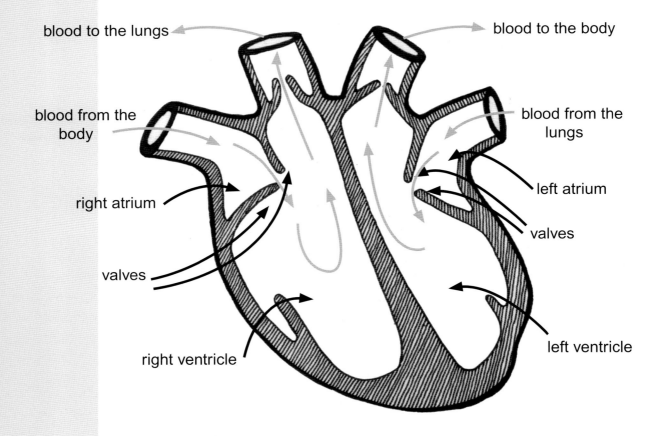

*Interesting heart facts*
- ♥ A baby's heart beats about 120 times a minute. This slows down as we get older — an adult's heart beats about 70 times every minute.
- ♥ Your heart is about the size of your fist.
- ♥ The fantastic trip your blood makes, from heart to lungs and back to heart again, then out to the body and back to the heart again, takes about 23 seconds!
- ♥ You can feel your heartbeat at pulse points in your body such as your neck and wrists.

# A mouse hunt!
### Friday 1.30 pm

I made it to the lobby at exactly 1.30 pm. Mum was pleased to see me because she was finding it hard to sit still for so long and concentrate on the people talking at the conference.

I could sympathise. I have great difficulty sitting still in class sometimes. If I have a seat by the window and I can see blue sky and white clouds, I'm lost! Especially in science with boring Mr Sinclair.

There's a park opposite the hotel. (This is the 'leafy outskirts' written about in the hotel brochure.) We bought sandwiches at a little shop and ate them in the park. Then Mum and I went for a gentle jog.

Mum needed to do this to keep awake for the next session, which was on report writing. Not writing school reports like 'Cherry could do better in science if she concentrated on the task', but writing information about different topics.

We met Anton and Helen coming out of the hotel just as we returned. They were on evening shifts this week and were going to the park for their break. They looked very miserable.

I introduced them to Mum, who gave them her commiserations. I had told Mum about their unhappy love affair during our jog. I told them not to lose heart — love always finds a way. They told Mum they would keep an eye on me, which made her happy.

I can see why Anton has fallen madly and passionately in love with Helen. She is absolutely stunning, even though she has big black rings under her eyes at the moment. I guess, from crying her heart out.

Mum went to her next writing session. I promised faithfully to keep out of trouble and meet her in our room at 6 pm.

Mum said it would be OK to go swimming in the hotel pool; otherwise I could watch TV in our room or do some homework. Would you believe it? Our English teacher Ms Honeywell has set homework for the holidays!

We have to find an interesting person and interview them about their job and why they like it. Then we have to write the interview as a journalism report.

Ms Honeywell doesn't know Mum, but I bet they would be good friends. They both love giving kids masses of homework.

I collected my swimming gear and went to explore the rooftop sauna, spa, gym and swimming pool.

There I met Joelene and Shane, the in-house gym instructors. They were expecting me because Mabel had told them to look out for me, which was very kind of her. Joelene and Shane are so cool. The rooftop gym, spa, sauna and swimming pool are excellent. They look just as good in real life as in the hotel brochure.

Joelene gave me a fitness test. She said I was very fit and could use the state-of-the-art gym equipment whenever I like. I just have to be careful not to hog the equipment if the gym is full of business people — mainly in the mornings and at night.

Joelene said business people really need to use the gym and spa to de-stress themselves. I can understand this: I feel stressed keeping out of trouble! Joelene said to bring Mum to the gym too — it will be good for Mum after sitting still through so many writing sessions.

It was a quiet time in the gym. Shane said he would hold the fort while Joelene showed me around the hotel. We could look for mice at the same time.

Mabel is unsure whether or not to report the murdered mouse to Winston, the guest relations manager. Everyone advised Mabel to wait and see if another mouse shows up. Winston is a bit of a worrier; he could have the hotel crawling with pest exterminators before you could say boo. It would be terrible if the hotel was invaded by pest exterminators for nothing.

Joelene gave me a very interesting tour of the hotel. It is enormous. There are floors and floors of nothing but deep-pile carpeted halls with rooms opening off them.

She introduced me to lots of hotel workers, which was very kind of her.

I loved the mezzanine floor. It was kind of a half-floor built over the lobby. The Park Cafe is situated on the mezzanine floor. It provides 'casual eating in a warm Mediterranean atmosphere'. I also met Joe, the Park Cafe Manager. Joe said I could have an on-the-house (free) hot chocolate any time.

Joe also plays piano in the Park Lounge at night, and sometimes on a Sunday, when they serve lavish afternoon teas.

He said Mum and I should come and listen to him play. It's free entry but you have to pay for drinks.

Joe says he would definitely prefer to play piano all the time, but there isn't enough money in it. He said I was very welcome to perch in the Park Cafe any time and watch the celebrities in the lobby below.

The hotel has some absolutely gorgeous shops. They are really, really expensive. Very handy for some guests, but not suitable for Mum and me. We have to keep to a tight budget.

I was introduced to James the concierge, and Jess, who sells flowers in Park Flowers. James arranges trips and other services for guests. Jess gave us a big bunch of red roses to take back to George, the houseman — housekeepers are called 'housemen' if they are male. The roses are for the hotel's 'Runaway Indulgent Weekends'.

These are special deals the hotel does for weekends. Everyone gets red roses and chocolates on their pillows and other stuff at bargain prices.

I also met Trish, who works in the Park Hair Salon. Trish said I could come for a free fringe trim anytime. I decided to take her up on her offer tomorrow.

Joelene and I checked out the basement for mice. I met Henry, one of the hotel valets. He parks cars for the 'complimentary undercover, security car parking' mentioned in the Hotel Directory.

The basement was quite spooky — an excellent place for a murder. I took notes for my murder mystery.

I checked to see if our car was OK. We had only had it for a few weeks. Mum and Grandma Cheng wrote a book called *The Golden Dragon Cookbook*. It's been a best seller. Mum bought our car with her royalties. Grandma spent her royalty money on an overseas holiday to visit our relatives in China, Hong Kong and San Francisco.

The hotel keeps bicycles in the basement for guests to use. I made a note to tell Mum. But there was no sign of any spare mice.

Joelene and I dropped the roses off to George, then returned to the rooftop pool. I had a sauna, swim and spa and was back in my room by 6 pm.

Mum arrived right on time. We went out for hamburgers and bought a supply of fruit and healthy food snacks. I renewed my promise not to eat any hotel-provided snacks from the fridge.

Meals are included in the conference price, but Mum likes to eat with me. Tomorrow night is the big conference dinner so Mum is going to that. Mum said I could order my dinner from Room Service and watch a video.

I sent faxes to Grandma and Grant.


*PS Grant is not my boyfriend. He is a good friend who happens to be a boy!*

(Story continues on page 25.)

## FACSIMILE TRANSMISSION SHEET

| Country | Code | Area Code | Fax Number |
|---------|------|-----------|------------|
|         |      |           |            |

**To:** Lily Cheng
**From:** Cherry Cheng
**No of pages (including this sheet):** 1

**Message**
Dear Grandma
Day one trouble free! Fantastic hotel!
Love and kisses
Cherry


Cherry Cheng
**Date 21 May**
**Room 541**
**Time 6 pm**

**To:** Grant McKenna
**From:** Cherry Cheng
**No of pages (including this sheet):** 1

**Message**
Dear Grant
This hotel is cool. Just like on TV and in the movies. I was nearly involved in a murder but everything is OK now.
In-line skates looking good.
Regards
Cherry

Cherry Cheng
**Date 21 May**
**Room 541**
**Time 6.05 pm**

# How to write an advertisement

Advertisements are a type of persuasive writing. They should contain brief, catchy information and be attractive and well designed. There are different kinds of advertisements, including display and classified advertisements. The sample below is a display advertisement for the Grand Hotel's 'Runaway Indulgent Weekends'. (I helped Mabel put chocolates and roses in the rooms. I think the packages are a good deal if you have someone romantic to be with, ie not your mother.) Classified advertisements like 'for sale', 'for rent' and 'wanted' are shorter.

# How to write a report

People write reports to organise and record information on a topic. Reports usually have two parts — a general classification and a description. You can write reports that classify and describe almost anything, for example bikes, telephones, mountains or trees.
It seems to me that students are usually asked to write reports to describe almost anything in absolutely every subject … so it's a good idea to know how to write one. This is my sample report on mice. Mice have been on my mind ever since the murder.

## Mice

Part 1 general classification → Mice are small, furry animals with long tails. They belong to a group of mammals called 'rodents'.

Part 2 description (related facts) → Rodents have two large front teeth and two bottom teeth for gnawing food. Most mice are omnivorous (they eat both animal and plant foods such as insects, seeds, fruit and grasses.

Mice have two small ears, a blunt nose with whiskers, and two small black eyes. They have strong chewing muscles and cheek pouches for carrying food. They have four legs.

comparison — There are many different kinds of mice. House mice are the (most common). Harvest mice are the (smallest). The (average) mouse is 150–180 millimetres long, and weighs 15–28 grams.

Mice live in most parts of the world except Antarctica.

action words — Mice are born bald, blind and deaf. They (hide) in their nest until they are about two weeks old and begin (exploring). Then the young mice become

linking words and phrases — covered with hair. (After three weeks) young mice stop feeding on their mother's milk. (After six weeks) they are ready to live on their own and start breeding.

Mice breed at a very fast rate. They are often a nuisance to people because they eat and destroy food and crops.

## A FRAMEWORK FOR WRITING REPORTS

Reports are divided into two main parts — *general classification* and *description*.

**General classification**
Begin with a general classification, for example, *Mice are mammals*. Use words that are general. Talk about *mice,* not a particular mouse such as the harvest mouse, or Manuel Mouse.

**Description**
The description should be made up of a logical sequence of facts. Use mainly present tense verbs like *is, are, happens, works*. Don't use first person pronouns (*I, we*) or write your own opinion, eg *I think mice are very cute animals*.
The description section of a report can be organised in many ways — alphabetical order, case studies, scientific categories, cause and effect, compare and contrast, question and answer, and so on.

**Summary**
Reports don't usually have an ending like a story, but you can round them off with a general statement if you like.

# Handy hints
## *Handy hints for writing reports*

- Reports should be clear and factual. Don't fill them with irrelevant details or personal opinions.
- Use factual and precise words rather than imaginative or emotional adjectives. For example, write *soft* fur not *cuddly* fur.
- Classification (*belong to, are a member of*) and compare and contrast (*are similar to*, *smaller than*, *like a*) help to set the picture and clarify what you are talking about.
- *Visual thinking* helps you get good ideas for reports and other writing. Use a diagram of small quick sketches or words, and written ideas to help organise your thinking and information.

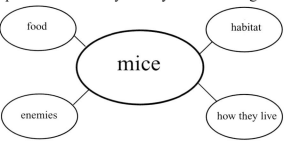

23

# Scientific name: *Mus musculus* — House mouse

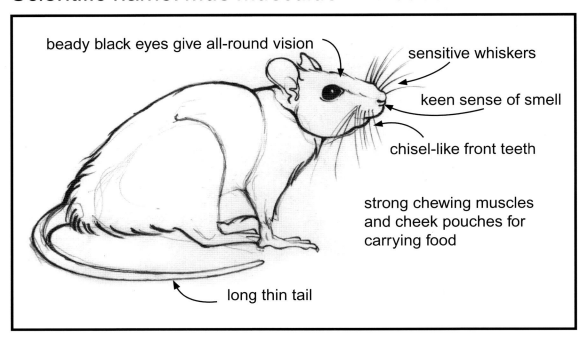

## Interesting mice facts

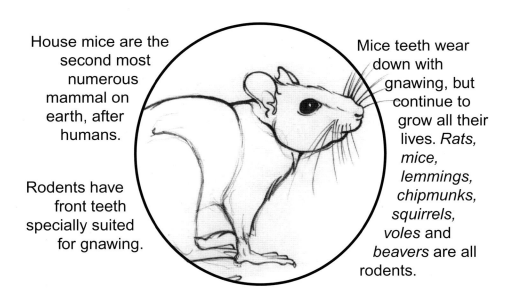

House mice are the second most numerous mammal on earth, after humans.

Rodents have front teeth specially suited for gnawing.

Mice teeth wear down with gnawing, but continue to grow all their lives. *Rats, mice, lemmings, chipmunks, squirrels, voles* and *beavers* are all rodents.

## Trouble again!
### Saturday 9.00 am

We were woken by a knocking on our door. (I told Mum she should have let me order a wake-up call!) Alma, a lovely room service attendant, brought our breakfast. They do a sumptuous buffet breakfast in the Park Dining Room, but it is cheaper to have a continental breakfast in your room and fill up on fruit if you get hungry.

Guests are given a neat Breakfast Choosing Menu to mark and leave on the door handle of their room. The breakfast orders are collected at night, before 2 am. A room service attendant delivers your breakfast at the time you request it. Cool!

Mum dashed off to a recount writing session. Recount writing is so basic. As long as I can remember, I have been writing recounts in school — you know, retelling something like *The best thing that happened in the holidays* — stuff like that.

I had to meet her in the lobby at 1.30, then we were going for a sandwich in the park.

I loved the interactive TV in the Grand Hotel. You could send and receive messages, as well as being able to watch masses of channels — but you had to pay to watch videos.

After I had finished watching *News of the world,* I decided to have a bubble bath. The Grand Hotel provides guests with cute little bottles of bubble bath — absolutely free!

That was when trouble reared its ugly head!

I have written a sample recount of this near disaster. Read on!

(Story continues on page 28.)

# How to write a recount

A recount text is writing that tells of past experiences or events. It is arranged in chronological order — the sequence of time that the events happened. It can be personal, factual or imaginary.

**Stranded practically naked!**
**(A near tragic tale by Cherry Cheng)**

*when* — *who*

It was Saturday morning. We were staying in the Grand Hotel because my mum was at the English Teachers' Conference. I finished breakfast and decided to have a bubble bath. I was just about to leap into a deep, luxurious bath filled to the brim with frothy bubbles when I remembered that I had forgotten to put our breakfast tray outside the door.

*why* — Mabel says it makes things easy for the housekeepers if guests do this. It is written on the breakfast menu: *Please place breakfast tray outside door when finished.* Mabel says it's amazing how many people forget to do this.

*events in sequence* — I grabbed a towel and wrapped it around me, picked up our breakfast tray and opened the door. I lowered the tray carefully onto the floor when my towel slipped. I grabbed my towel. Then the door slammed shut behind me! Bang!

I was locked outside our room. Stranded! Only a towel between me and the rest of the world. I could see my state-of-the-art in-line skates sprouting wings and floating off into the distance.

*use of pronouns*
*This recount is written in the first person — it's about me, so I used the personal pronoun* I *a lot.*

I looked around me. No one in sight.
Don't panic, don't panic! I told myself. I sat down beside our breakfast tray and thought.

If I sneaked into the back of the conference room, could I attract Mum's attention without other delegates seeing me?

No way.

Could I leave a telephone message for Mum at the reception desk?

Not possible. There wasn't a telephone in sight and I didn't have any loose change in my pocket. I didn't even have a pocket.

Then I had a brainwave. I would go to the rooftop gym and spa and stay there beside the pool, wrapped in my towel until Mum finished her session. Joelene or Shane could locate Mum for me.

I gathered my towel around me. Thank goodness it was a big one! I walked nonchalantly along the hall to the lift and waited.

Eventually the lift arrived and the door opened. There was Mabel with her service trolley. I've never been so pleased to see someone in all my life.

Mabel opened our room. She said I wouldn't have been able to operate the lift. The computerised encoded VingCard that opens our door also operates the lift. Modern hotels are very safety conscious, which is comforting if you are a wealthy tourist dripping with jewels.

*events in sequence* → After I had finished my bubble bath, I got dressed and met Mabel in the staffroom for a calming cup of tea.

Mabel introduced me to Gloria, the conference facilitator for Mum's English Teachers' Conference. She is in charge of the hotel's conference facilities and helps organise the conferences.

*summary comment* → Gloria and Mabel said that people get locked out of rooms quite often — even famous people — and not to worry about it.

I decided not to tell Mum. She would worry and not be able to concentrate on the conference, which would be a waste of money!

## A FRAMEWORK FOR WRITING RECOUNTS

This framework can help you with your planning when you are writing a recount.

**Beginning**

Write a quick introduction for the reader explaining the setting and time of the event you are recounting. It should answer *who*, *when* and *where*.

**Middle**

Write a series of events in sequence, ie in order of time they happened.

**End**

Writing at the end can include personal opinions, observations, comments or findings.

# Handy hints for writing recounts

- Use past tense verbs like *grabbed, wrapped, walked, met, sneaked*.
- Use words like *meanwhile, during, later, simultaneously, eventually, gradually, after, before*, and *then* to explain events in the order they happened.

## A free fringe trim
### Saturday 11.30 am

I had planned to have a swim in the rooftop pool. But I decided I had seen enough of water, so I went to visit Trish in the Park Hair Salon. Trish had had a cancellation, so she gave me a free fringe trim.

She was an excellent hairdresser, and said I had lovely hair. I told Trish I used to hate my hair. I wanted hair like my best friend Tammy. Tammy's hair is blonde and curly. Mine is black, straight and very thick, which is understandable because I'm half-Chinese.

My dad, John Cheng, was Chinese and had hair like mine. He was killed in a car accident when I was a baby. I can't remember him at all — we only have photographs, but he looks like Grandma. Mum is Australian and changes the colour of her hair a lot.

Grandma Cheng says I have the best of both my parents, which is nice, but my hair definitely comes from Grandma Cheng and my dad.

Trish and I swapped childhood memories. I told Trish I hated school because bullies were always out to get me. Then Tammy arrived and became my best friend. Tammy was the new kid when I was in Grade 2 and Ms Jones sat her next to me. Tammy looks as if she couldn't hurt a flea, but she's ferocious!

As soon as Tammy took me under her wing, kids stopped bullying me. I have never met anyone who can return name-calling as well as Tammy — she's dynamite. Tammy says it's probably because she had plenty of practice with her five brothers.

When we were little we shared our lunches — noodles, dumplings, and cheese sandwiches. Tammy has always loved my mum's and Grandma Cheng's cooking. On the way home from school we often call at Grandma Cheng's and she cooks noodles for us. Tammy's mum works shift work. She is a terrible cook.

Grandma Cheng says you should be comfortable with who you are and not worry about other people. This is fine now I'm at high school, but it was hard when I was in the junior grades.

Trish says practically everyone who comes into the salon wishes for different hair. I told Trish I was quite comfortable with my hair now, especially as Tammy and my other friends would just die for long, black, straight hair.

After my free fringe trim I went to the Park Cafe on the mezzanine floor and chatted with Joe. He gave me a free hot chocolate and said there was a TV soap celebrity in the hotel — but I couldn't spot her.

I did spot Anton in the lobby and raced downstairs to talk to him. He was waiting for Helen; they were going to see Helen's parents once again to try to talk them into agreeing to the wedding. I told Anton he should never give up his quest to marry Helen. Otherwise they could end up like the lovers Koong-se and Chang in a Chinese folk tale Grandma used to tell me when I was little.

Anton thanked me for my support. I hope Anton smiles a lot when he talks to Helen's parents. He has a heart-melting smile.

I returned to the Park Cafe and chatted to Joe. I told him that for my homework I had to interview someone I met on holidays. Joe suggested I interview Carlo, the new executive chef at the Grand Hotel. I might just do that this afternoon.

I saw Mum in the lobby and dashed down to meet her — 1.30 on the dot!

So far so good! In my mind I could see Tammy and Grant skating along the track at home, and I was right behind them on my very own state-of-the-art in-line skates.

I hoped Anton and Helen would be able to talk Helen's parents into agreeing to their marriage. What a tragic life they would lead if Helen's parents didn't relent.

(Story continues on page 34.)

# How to write a narrative

A narrative is writing that tells a story. There are many different kinds of narrative texts:

- modern realistic stories
- traditional tales — fables, folk tales, fairy tales, myths, legends, pourquoi tales
- animal stories
- humorous stories
- mysteries
- science fiction
- historical fiction

## A FRAMEWORK FOR WRITING NARRATIVES

Different kinds of narrative writing usually follow the same structure.
*(Make a plan before you start writing and you can't go wrong!)*

**Orientation**
Introduce characters and setting.
- *Who* are the characters?
- *When* and *where* does the story take place?

**Complication**
Write a sequence of events.
- *What* is the story about?
- *What* is the problem/conflict of the story?
- *How* do the characters try to solve the problem?

**Crisis**
The complication becomes very dramatic.

**Resolution**
*How* is the problem/conflict solved?
*What* is the outcome for the characters?

♥ The following narrative sample is the tragic love story I told Anton about. It's a traditional tale.

# The story of the willow pattern

In the days when China was ruled by emperors, there was a wealthy mandarin named Ta-jin. He had a beautiful daughter called Koong-se. They lived in a grand house by a swift flowing river, edged with weeping willow trees. Koong-se had everything her heart desired — except happiness.

One day a humble clerk called Chang came to work at her father's grand house. Chang and Koong-se fell instantly in love with each other.

When Ta-jin discovered Chang and Koong-se were in love, he forbade Koong-se to ever see Chang again. He ordered his servants to build new quarters for Koong-se. A bridge across the river was Koong-se's only escape from her quarters.

Ta-jin arranged for Koong-se to marry an old widower, who was his friend, as soon as the peach blossom bloomed.

Koong-se was heartbroken. She watched the buds on the peach tree. She dreaded the day they would bloom and she would have to marry the old widower.

However, Chang remained steadfast in his love for Koong-se. He sent secret messages and poems to her in coconut shells, which floated on the river.

On the night before the wedding of Koong-se to the old widower, the house was full of bustle. Chang entered Koong-se's quarters in disguise and the two lovers escaped across the bridge.

Ta-jin chased after them but Koong-se's faithful handmaiden had hidden a boat for their escape. They floated down the river to freedom.

Koong-se and Chang lived happily together on an island for many years. They had sons who grew up and went away to study with a great scholar. Chang became famous throughout the land as a poet and writer.

Ta-jin came to hear of Chang because of his poetry and books. Ta-jin wanted revenge and sent his soldiers to kill Chang and bring Koong-se back to him.

The soldiers found Chang and killed him. Koong-se witnessed this dreadful deed and full of despair, ran back into their house. She set the house on fire and perished with it.

The gods looked down and cursed Ta-jin for his cruelty. He died soon after, a sad and lonely old man.

The gods rewarded the two lovers for their undying and steadfast love. Their spirits were transformed into two doves and the two doves live together for ever in peace and happiness.

## Interesting information

The blue and white willow pattern has been printed since 1780 on china dinner sets.

If you look carefully at the willow pattern design, you can see Koong-se and Chang being chased by Ta-jin over the bridge as the two lovers escape. You can also see the willow tree weeping over the river, the mandarin's house, the bridge, the peach tree and two doves flying in perfect peace and freedom together.

PS
Please don't write to my publishers about my murder mystery not having an ending. Read page 56 for the resolution of the mouse mystery.
C. Cheng

## The Carlo Interview
### Saturday 2.30 pm

I dashed down to the Dining Room to see if Anton and Helen were back with any good news. They weren't. But, as luck would have it, Carlo, the executive chef (boss of all the hotel's restaurants) was having a cup of coffee in the kitchen with Winston, the guest relations manager.

I asked Carlo if I could interview him. I told him I had my questions ready so it wouldn't take too long.

Carlo said he was very happy to oblige. He wasn't grumpy at all. Helen had said that Carlo was like a bear with a sore head sometimes — especially if the cooks messed up his menus.

Carlo and Winston invited me to join them for a cup of coffee. Winston was a jumpy person — I could see what Mabel and the other staff meant when they said Winston was very nervy and panicked easily. I told him he should de-stress at the rooftop gym.

We chatted about cooking. I told Carlo and Winston I had been brought up with cooking — Mum had worked with Grandma Cheng in the Golden Dragon ever since I was little. She needed to earn money to go to university to become an English teacher.

Carlo said the Golden Dragon has an excellent reputation, which was good to hear, and that he had read Grandma and Mum's book *The Golden Dragon Cookbook*. He liked the recipes very much. Carlo likes to incorporate an Asian flavour into his cooking too.

I'm going to fax Grandma and ask for her recipe for 'Crab with Chilli Sauce' — Carlo's favourite food. I'm sure she won't mind.

Winston asked me to make sure I fill in the Guest Evaluation Questionnaire.

I said I rated the Grand Hotel as superior deluxe — bordering on perfection. The only thing missing was wildlife. Other than a few pigeons and the goldfish in the Palm Courtyard, the hotel was bare of wildlife.

I didn't mention the five-letter word beginning with *m*.

I enjoyed interviewing Carlo, and added 'reporter' to my future possible career list.

Winston and Carlo knew about Anton and Helen's heartbreaking story, and were sad for them. Carlo also knew about the English Teachers' Conference dinner, which was being held that night. He helped the chefs to plan the menu. I told him I was having room-service sandwiches and watching TV while Mum was at the dinner.

Carlo and Winston invited me to dine in the Park Dining Room — compliments of the hotel. Winston said he would contact Mum to arrange formal permission.

I couldn't stop thinking about Anton and Helen's quest for love. I was dying to hear if the wedding was going ahead.

(Story continues on page 42.)

# THE GRAND HOTEL
## ON THE PARK

## EXPECTING MESSAGE FORM

If you are leaving your room and expect a message or visitor, please fill in this form and hand it to the reception desk.

**Name:** Cherry Cheng
**Room:** 541
**Date:** 22/5/2001

**I will be at (please tick):**

- ☐ Lobby
- ☐ Park Cafe
- ☐ Park Dining Room
- ☐ Palm Courtyard
- ☐ Conference Room
- ☐ Rooftop pool
- ☐ Rooftop gym

**Time**
From: _____  To: _____

# How to write news reports from interviews

Journalists often interview people to get information for a report. There are a few tricks to doing good interviews.

**The interview**
- Prepare questions.
- Find a quiet place for your interview.
- Look at the person you are interviewing and make sure they can hear you.
- Listen carefully.
- Be prepared to ask a question in a different way if the person you are interviewing doesn't understand your question the first time.
- Take notes or use a tape recorder. (I took notes and typed up my interview later using the hotel's conference facilities )
- Make sure the information is accurate, easy to understand and interesting.

**Questions I asked Carlo**
- How long have you been a chef?
- Where did you learn to cook?
- What kind of food do you like to cook?
- How did you get the job at the Grand Hotel?
- Do you think being a chef is a good career?

I wrote the newspaper report opposite from my interview with Carlo.

# Handy hints for writing a news report

Begin with the most important information.
- *Who* or *what* is the report about?

Follow the introduction with a series of facts about the subject.
- Don't go into too much detail with each fact.
- Keep the paragraphs short. Each paragraph is about a different fact.

Include quotations from the interview if they are suitable.

# A Grand Executive Chef!

## by Cherry Cheng

**Carlo Tarantino is the new executive chef at the Grand Hotel. He was headhunted from a famous five-star Italian hotel.**

Under Carlo's careful guidance, the Grand Hotel's three dining areas offer patrons the best food in town.

Carlo brings with him a wealth of knowledge and experience.

He has worked in the finest restaurants in Europe and Asia, and has also been part of a successful culinary team that competed in the Cooking Olympics held in Europe.

As a young seventeen-year-old cook, he worked in kitchens with tough, temperamental chefs. 'This was a good training ground and very character building,' he says.

Carlo calls himself a 'food doctor'. He coordinates the 17 hotel chefs. They use the freshest ingredients that are low in fats and oil, but high in flavour, to create healthy, culinary masterpieces for diners.

Cooking is a very exciting, creative and satisfying career.

'More young people should think about becoming chefs,' says Carlo.

# How to write a procedural text

A procedural text is writing that explains how to do something through a sequence of actions or steps. Procedural texts are also called 'how-to' texts or 'instruction' texts. My sample procedural text is a Golden Dragon recipe.

## Stir-fry Chinese vegetables

*From the kitchen of the Golden Dragon!*
This recipe comes adapted and simplified so you can try it at home. Make sure you use fresh vegetables. You don't have to stick to these particular vegetables. A combination of five different kinds is fine.

Preparation time: 15 minutes
Total cooking time: 7 minutes
Serves 4

### Ingredients
300 g (2 or 3) bok choy (Chinese cabbage)
1 medium carrot
150 g (4¾ oz) broccoli
1 medium onion
1 medium red pepper (capsicum)
2 tablespoons cooking oil
2 cloves of crushed garlic
2 teaspoons grated ginger
1 tablespoon (extra) sesame oil
2 teaspoons soy sauce

### Method
1. Wash the bok choy and trim away thick stalks. Cut the leaves into wide strips.
2. Cut carrot into thin slices. Cut the onion into thin wedges. Cut the broccoli into small florets and the red pepper into strips.
3. Heat the oil in a large frying pan or wok. Add garlic and ginger and cook over medium heat for 30 seconds, stirring constantly.
4. Add the carrot, onion and broccoli, and stir-fry for 3 minutes.
5. Add the pepper, stir-fry for 2 more minutes, then add the bok choy and stir for 1 more minute.
6. Stir in the (extra) sesame oil and soy sauce, and toss through.
Serve immediately with boiled rice or noodles.

## FRAMEWORK FOR WRITING A PROCEDURAL TEXT

Procedural texts follow a definite form — especially recipes.

**Title**

Name of procedure (eg recipe)

**Introduction**

This is usually a short description of what the activity is about and why it might be interesting to do.

**List of items needed**

In a recipe, the items needed are called *ingredients*. They are written in a list.

**Instructions**

- The instructions are usually written as a series of steps needed to carry out the activity. In a recipe, they are often written under the heading *method*.
- The instructions are often numbered so you don't do them in the wrong order.
- The sentences are usually commands. (Do this. Don't do that.)

# Handy hints

*Handy hint for making Stir-fry Chinese Vegetables*

You can cut carrots and other vegetables into shapes like dragons etc. In the restaurant we use little cutting dies, which makes it easy.

**Interesting fact**
There are many kinds of Chinese cabbage. Bok choy (or choi) has thick white stalks all joined at the base and dark green leaves.
— Lily Cheng

## How to write an email

Email is a very quick and cheap way to send messages without having to worry about envelopes and stamps. It costs the same as a local phone call to send an email message and takes only a few minutes for a message to reach its destination anywhere in the world.

1. Use a computer that has an email program.
2. Open the email program on the computer.
3. Click on *New Message* (or *Compose Message*) to type a new message.
4. Click in the *Address* box and type in the email address of the person you are sending your email to.
5. Type the title of your email message in the *Subject* box.
6. Click in the main box and type your message.
7. Click on the *Send* button to send the message.

## Handy hints for writing an email

- Be brief.
- Send messages in a plain font; flashy fonts are hard to read.
- Check the message you are sending, and that you have addressed it correctly. The wrong email to the wrong person can be deadly!
- Check your spelling and grammar. If your email is worth writing, it's worth writing well! (Advice from Mum and Ms Honeywell.)
- Be careful what information you give in emails. Don't include a signature that has your home address or telephone number on emails to strangers.

**This is an email I sent to Tammy.**

| | |
|---|---|
| To : | Tammy@ .com |
| Cc: | |
| Subject: | In-line skates |

Date:
From: Cherry Cheng < 541@thegrandhotel.com.au>
>
Message
>
Dear Tammy
>
Survived two days and one night. In-line skates looking good.
>
See you soon.
Love
Cherry

## Fine dining
### Saturday 6.00 pm

There were two messages waiting for us on the interactive television screen in our room. Porters sometimes bring messages to your room too.

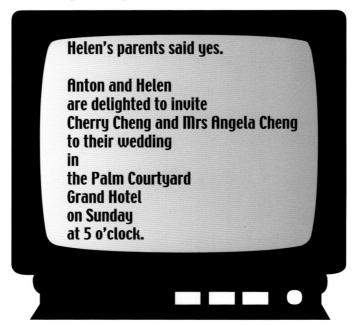

Helen's parents said yes.

Anton and Helen
are delighted to invite
Cherry Cheng and Mrs Angela Cheng
to their wedding
in
the Palm Courtyard
Grand Hotel
on Sunday
at 5 o'clock.

Awesome!
    Mum and I were very happy for Anton and Helen. Mum said we would definitely stay for the wedding.
    There were two writing sessions on Sunday and an 'end-of-it-all party' for conference delegates.
    Mum said lots of people would probably have to leave the conference early to catch planes, trains etc, so it wouldn't matter if she slipped out to go to the wedding.
    We decided that I would pack our bags and stow them in the car. Then we would be able to dash away after the wedding. We didn't want to put up our tent in the dark, and Mum hates sleeping in the car.
    I was so glad Grandma Cheng made me pack one respectable outfit. Grandma says it always pays to be prepared.
    Mum was happy for me to dine in the Park Dining Room.

    Eating in the Park Dining Room was unbelievably excellent. The food was dazzling. There were five courses. Anton waited at my table — he had the biggest grin on his face all night. He practically danced around the tables as he served people.

Helen made me the most scrumptious dessert I have ever eaten. It was a five-star edible extravaganza — icecream, fruit, cake and cream, all covered in a cage of toffee. Yummy!

Mum collected me after the conference dinner. She was giving her paper (a talk of about 60 minutes) in the morning.

She practised on me before we went to sleep. I had to listen and watch in case she said any ums or ahs, twiddled with her buttons or picked her nose etc.

I think it must have been the 1000th time I listened to Mum reading her paper.

I dreamt about my state-of-the-art in-line skates and trendy skate gear.

One more day and they would be mine! Yes!

# A life-threatening dilemma
## Sunday 9.00 am

Mum was in a flat panic because she was delivering her paper at the next writing session. I told her not to worry, she'd be great! She'd certainly rehearsed enough. Everything Mum needed to know would be on the computer and the overhead projector. (She was doing a multimedia presentation.)

The only problem I could see was if she couldn't answer questions at the end of her session. I told Mum to tell the teachers to stay behind and see her later if they have questions. Our teachers do this all the time, and no one ever stays behind to miss recess.

After Mum left, I checked her list of things to do.

### Sunday morning

1. Wash and dry clothes in guest laundry.
2. Pack bags.
3. Deposit bags in car.
4. Finish homework!
5. Meet in hotel lobby at 1.30 for lunch.

I checked the Hotel Directory to locate the laundry. We needed a clean start for our camping trip.

I collected our dirty washing and stepped onto our balcony for one last breathtaking city view.

I jumped up and down to get a complete view and dropped our dirty washing. It fell over the balcony, straight down into the Palm Courtyard!

Most of our washing was caught on the palms. Mum's best superbra dropped into the feature waterfall. A pair of my knickers fell into the fishpond!

Great. Trouble with a capital T!
Mum would be furious. Mega furious!

If I didn't do something quickly, the whole world would see our dirty washing decorating the palms in the Palm Courtyard when they came to Helen and Anton's wedding.

While Tammy and Grant rollerbladed I would be running behind them for the rest of my life.

Something had to be done. Immediately!

I needed help quickly.

I took the lift to the staffroom.

Gloria the conference facilitator was there. She was putting her feet up, having a cup of coffee. She felt the English Teachers' Conference had been a great success, even though there was still a bit to go.

I told her my desperate plight. Should I ring the fire department? Would they be able to help? Gloria was so cool and comforting.

Truly this hotel has been full of the coolest, kindest people.

Gloria rang Harry from the maintenance department. He said he would meet us in the Palm Courtyard.

Harry had a huge extension ladder that they used to put up the lights and decorations for functions. Gloria and I held the bottom of the ladder. Harry climbed up, unhooked our washing and dropped it down to us below.

I have never been so glad to see dirty washing in my whole life.

Then he directed me so I could collect Mum's superbra from the feature waterfall and my knickers from the fishpond. I checked for fish.

I stuffed our washing into my pockets and up my windcheater and caught the lift to the guest laundry.

Once the washing was whirling around in the machine I relaxed.

Fellow hotel guests, Simon and Rachel, were also doing their washing. They were really interesting people and had led adventurous lives travelling all over the world.

We chatted about famous cities until our washing was dry and folded. No way was I letting it out of my sight again.

Then I raced back to our room to check Mum's list.

I had to do my homework. Gloria was an angel and let me use the facilities in the business centre.

I could hardly concentrate because my mind was on the wedding. I hoped it would go smoothly.

I had never actually been to a wedding before. Tammy and I had watched wedding parties getting their photos taken at the Clifton Gardens, but that is not the same as being invited to a wedding.

I packed our gear, raced to the underground security car park, stuffed our bags into our car and met Mum in the lobby with a minute to spare. We bought sandwiches and walked around the park.

Mum was happy because her presentation had gone really well!

I didn't think it was necessary to trouble Mum with the plight of our dirty washing. It would probably dampen her spirits.

I saw Mum off to her last writing session — it was on poetry.

There was a message on the TV screen when I returned to our room.

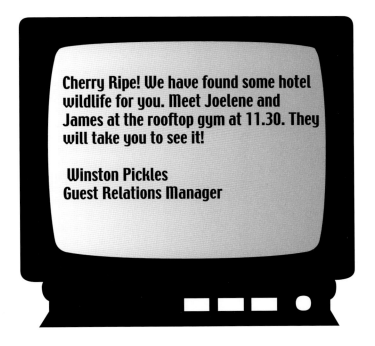

(Story continues on page 50.)

# How to write poetry

You can make poetry do what you like. Poems can be any shape, size or form and about anything.

Writing poetry is not my thing! In fact I find writing poetry is pure torture. Tammy, my best friend, absolutely loves writing poetry. She says poetry comes from the heart. Every spare minute she is putting her thoughts on paper in poetic form.

Mum and Grandma Cheng say there is poetry in everybody. Grant and I doubt there is poetry in us! I have included handy hints for writers who have trouble writing poetry. Please note the torture I have been through to get this poetry out of me.

The sample below is your most basic type of poem or verse. Anton sent this poem to Helen with a bunch of red roses. Helen says he has written much better romantic poems but they do not want them published.

P.S. I don't think you would get a good mark for poems like this.

Roses are red,
Violets are blue,
If you were a star,
I would wish for you.

An *acrostic poem* is a good way to get started on writing poetry. Choose a word. Write the letters vertically. Add more words that describe the word. Obviously mice were on my mind while we were at the hotel!

### Mouse
**M**ammal
**O**ut and about!
**U**nder here! Under there!
**S**cissor sharp teeth
**E**ating anything.

*Shape poems* are poems that take the shape of their subjects.

*An epitaph*

*Poor little mouse.*
*Squashed dead*
*Under Mabel's foot.*
*Rest In Peace.*

Poetry is about finding words that rhyme, or sound interesting. I wrote 'Hearts' to give you an idea on using words around one theme. (I couldn't get love and hearts off my mind during our stay in the Grand Hotel). Mum helped me a bit. Once you get going I have to admit you can get into the swing of writing poetry and it's not too bad.

## Hearts

*Heartfelt*
*Heart beat!*
*Young heart! Brave heart!*
*Hearts young and free.*
*The Queen of Hearts*
*The King of Hearts*
*Loving hearts! Sweethearts!*
*The Jack of Hearts*
*Heartless*
*Heartbreak! Heartache!*
*Hearts full of sorrow!*
*Heartburn!*
*Heart attack!*
*Heart surgery!*
*Happy, healthy and hearty!*

— Cherry Cheng

### THE GOLDEN DRAGON RESTAURANT

Chinese lanterns hanging in a red room.
Lacquered screens,
Tables and chairs.
White starched table cloths,
Fan folded napkins.
Blue and white bowls and chopsticks.
A room buzzing with the sound of hungry people!
Fantastic smells.
Mouth-watering noodles.
Unleash a hundred secret senses.

— Cherry Cheng

# How to write notices, messages and memos

Notices, messages and memos are ways of communicating information. We have always been a note-writing family but never in my whole life have I seen so many notices, messages and memos as in this hotel. I collected some that were particularly useful and helpful.

Dear Guest

Can you imagine how many towels are washed unnecessarily in all the hotels and other accommodation around the world, and how much washing soaps and detergents pollute and burden our waters?
It's your decision. Towels on the rack mean you are happy to use them once more. Towels in the shower and spa bath mean please change them.
Thank you for that extra step in helping us promote a better environment.
This way staying at the Grand Hotel will never cost the earth!

This was a cross between a letter and a notice which was hung in our bathroom. I particularly approved of it. I was most impressed that the hotel cared about the environment too.

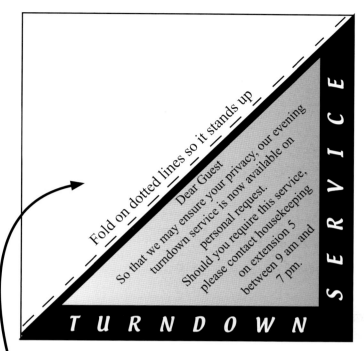

This notice was on our bed. We didn't need people to turn our beds down at night.

I found the Hotel Directory most useful. It was alphabetical and very handy.

We didn't use the babysitting or many other services the hotel offered.

James the concierge said he had arranged services for guests from sewing buttons on their clothes to finding them last-minute fancy-dress costumes!

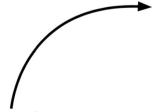

I thought this was a very polite notice to remind people to stop smoking.

# Hotel wildlife
## Sunday 12.00 pm

The Grand certainly had real wildlife. Secret wildlife — as well as the wildlife in the Palm Courtyard (pigeons, sparrows, fish and an occasional frog).

It had peregrine falcons. Peregrine falcons are the fastest animals on earth. They fly at 320 km per hour when they are diving to catch their prey.

Actually, I didn't really see any peregrine falcons, but James and Joelene showed me their nest and photographs of the female peregrine falcon when she was on the nest last year. The nest was an oblong steel box fastened to the side of the top of the hotel. (In the wild, peregrines nest in extremely high positions on cliffs and trees.)

Apparently a pair nested in the hotel's rooftop drainpipe two years ago. Unfortunately their eggs didn't hatch because they were flooded out. However, Winston, who is an avid birdwatcher, contacted peregrine falcon experts. Harry from the maintenance department built a suitable nest for the falcons — hoping they would return the next year. And they did.

That year the pair hatched their fledglings. Everyone was hoping they would return this year. They probably will because peregrine falcons are very loyal to their nesting site.

Only a few hotel staff know about the peregrine falcons. Too much publicity could spoil everything for the birds.

Harry and Winston have been keeping a record of the birds, which made really interesting reading.

Suddenly everyone realised the time and raced off to prepare for Anton and Helen's wedding. Nearly the whole hotel staff were going. Winston had organised a roster so everyone could be released at some time to be at the wedding.

I was really looking forward to it!

# The wedding!
## Sunday 5.00 pm

It looked like everyone was at a funeral when Mum and I walked into the Palm Courtyard for Anton and Helen's wedding.

Anton was shaking so much you would have thought he'd been stuck in a crevasse in Antarctica for two weeks.

Helen's dad (Mr Papadopolous) was like Zeus, the Greek god of thunder. He looked as if he would explode at any moment.

Mrs Papadopolous, Helen's mum, looked an absolute wreck. She was making a shocking noise. It was a combination of a long sniff, half a hiccup and a heartbreaking sob — over and over again. It was heart wrenching!

Helen was nowhere in sight.

Mum and I sidled over to Mabel, Fred and their kids. Mabel was the Matron of Honour, and looked wonderful in lilac satin. It was the first time I had seen her out of uniform. Fred was best man. He said his hired suit was killing him because Mabel had hired a size too small in the pants. They told us the problem was Helen. She was missing! No one had heard from Helen since she had gone to the dressmaker's to pick up her wedding dress.

Mabel said that Helen had lost weight during the last few weeks because she had been so unhappy. Her wedding dress was falling off her and needed to be altered.

Well, we waited and waited. Ten, twenty, thirty minutes. Joe was playing the piano frantically in the background. He just about drowned out Mrs Papadopolous.

Carlo and Winston were overseeing the finger food. They were very worried. Carlo said that at the rate people were eating, there wouldn't be any food left for the *real* eating part of the wedding. Winston was upset because he didn't think his roster would work.

Then after forty minutes — *forty minutes* — James from reception came racing in. He had a message from Helen: she was stranded. Her car had broken down on the bridge and she was stuck in a gigantic traffic jam.

Fred immediately sprang into action. Mabel says Fred is an action person. He hates standing around doing nothing. Fred grabbed Mr Papadopolous and Anton and they raced off to rescue Helen.

Mum, Mabel and I took Mrs Papadopolous to the powder room. Mrs Papadopolous washed her face. Mum helped redo her make-up. After Mabel got her a cup of good strong tea, Mrs Papadopolous started to perk up. She even smiled a bit.

We waited another half an hour and then Joe started to play 'Here comes the bride' very loudly.

Everyone clapped and cheered as Helen and Anton, Fred and Mr Papadopolous entered the Palm Courtyard.

Helen looked a bit wrecked, but still stunning — like a beautiful windswept princess in her white satin bejewelled dress. It was definitely worth the money.

Anton had stopped shaking and was smiling. He looked drop-dead gorgeous even though he was a bit dirty and oily. He wore his waiter's suit but with a different vest and tie.

After that things went quite smoothly — except for one nervous moment when Anton dropped Helen's ring. It rolled across the tiles and nearly went into the fishpond, but I sprinted and stopped it with my foot. Awesome!

Everyone clapped and cheered.

After the wedding ceremony, Anton made a fantastic groom's speech. It made me cry. He said he and Helen owed a deep debt of gratitude to a certain person (me), who had encouraged them not to give up on their quest for a happy life together. It was so cool.

Anton danced with me just before we left. As we danced past the feature fountain, waterfall and fishpond I explained my life-threatening dilemma with our dirty washing.

Anton and I agreed that if the diamond wedding ring had fallen into the fishpond it would have been gone forever — eaten by a fish or swished down the reticulated water system. Anton said he would have been paying off diamond rings for the rest of his life.

I was most impressed when Helen and Anton danced around the Palm Courtyard and guests pinned money onto their clothes. What a great custom!

Then Helen and Anton left on their honeymoon. They were taking my advice and going camping. As Helen and Anton said, when you work in a hotel you definitely don't want to spend your honeymoon in one.

Mum and I said goodbye to everyone. We didn't want to be too late when we arrived at the camping ground. Putting up tents by torchlight can be a bit tricky.

We swapped addresses with Helen, Anton, Mabel, Carlo, Winston, Trish, Harry, Joelene, Gloria and all the other great people we met at the hotel. I hoped we would catch up with them again.

If all the four-star hotels are like the Grand Hotel — and if you have to stay in one — I can guarantee you'll have a cool time.

Successful writing!

Cherry Cheng

PS: Don't forget to read my Quick Reference Section for extra stuff.

# Extra Poetry

(I couldn't put this poem earlier in the book for obvious reasons. CC)

**The Wedding**
by Cherry Cheng

Anton waited nervously.
The room was filled with guests.
But as we feared
The bride had not appeared.
Waiting! Waiting! Waiting!
Everyone was waiting!
Soft music filled the air,
Guests whispered — and waited.
Guests fidgeted — and waited!
The pianist began to play …
Here comes the bride.
Thank goodness …
Helen had arrived.


**The Mammal**
Scared, furry mammal
Scurrying through the house.
Please don't panic
It is only a mouse.


**Crying at Weddings**
Lots of people cry at weddings.
I don't now why
They cry.

The next two poems were written by my friend Tammy Bjork. She just loves writing poetry and I thank her for her permission to include them in my book.

**The Mouse**
**by Tammy Bjork**
Quickly scampering, scurrying and darting —
Not knowing when its last step might be.
Risks are taken for tonight's dinner and tomorrow's breakfast.
Approaching the death trap he treads carefully.
He has seen these demons in action on his best friend.
It takes years of practice to outsmart these monsters.
Rising on his back legs he wriggles his nose — looking for the scent of food
This afternoon it's a bit of muffin.
Imagine what his wife and children will say
when he walks through the mouse hole with a huge bit of muffin.
Easing back onto all fours, he gets closer to his uncertain death.
His beady eyes skim over the pantry for something to detonate this bomb.
Ah-haa! A bit of broken board.
Not looking where he is going he races immediately towards the wood.
Bang!

**Eternity**
**by Tammy Bjork**
I am too preoccupied
To notice the hundreds of eager eyes.
You are my distraction.
Your eyes skim over my face.
And your hands are sweaty in mine.
The final frontier awaits us.
But you are smiling.
A murmured voice breaks the short silence.
It's an old man's voice asking questions.
Your eyes drift off my face towards this man.
And your lips open.
I do.
Now it's my turn.
The man asks the question identical to yours.
I try not to be hesitant, so I answer quickly, but surely, I do.
Now you're part of me.
For eternity
And beyond.

# How to write a newspaper recount

Not all the writing in a newspaper is *report* writing. Many articles are actually *recounts* — when a journalist writes articles that recall events that have happened. Newspaper recounts need snappy headlines, and a lead or introduction which answers *who, what, when* and *where* in the first paragraph.

## Hotel Mice Mystery Solved

**Cherry Cheng**

**A mouse was found dead in the Grand Hotel on Saturday at 11 o'clock. It was believed to be the first of a mouse infestation, which might invade the city.**

After careful examination the mouse was discovered to have been a future pet of Oliver Brown, son of Mabel Brown, a room service person.

'I had no idea Oliver had a pet mouse on loan from a friend,' said Mabel. 'The poor little creature must have been in the pocket of my uniform or handbag, and I brought it with me to the hotel.'

Oliver Brown is getting two new mice as pets. One to give back to his friend and one to keep.

## A FRAMEWORK FOR WRITING A RECOUNT FOR A NEWSPAPER

A news recount uses an inverted pyramid style of writing.

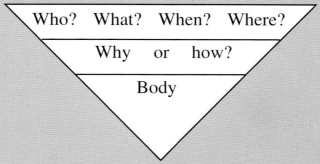

**Beginning**
The first paragraph should answer *who*, *what*, *where* and *when*.

**Middle**
The middle section should answer *why* or *how*.
Less important information is included at the end of the article.

# *Handy hints for writing a newspaper recount*

- Write in the third person (*he, she, it, they*). Do not use *I* or *me*.
- Write clearly and concisely.
- Use the past tense.

# Glossary

## Advertisement

Advertisements are persuasive writing. They should contain catchy, brief information and be attractive and well designed. There are different kinds of advertisements, for example *display* and *classified*.

## Ballad

A popular form of narrative poetry. Some modern ballads are folk, country or rock music. They are written in stanzas (verses) of four lines. The second and fourth lines are shorter and rhyme. They can have a chorus or refrain that is repeated. They often have direct speech.

## Crime fiction

Crime fiction is a popular form of narrative writing (see *narrative writing*). The essential elements of crime fiction are a crime, a detective or sleuth, suspects, clues and red herrings (false clues), and a solution. Crime fiction is also called detective, mystery, suspense fiction or whodunit.

## Diagrams, charts, graphs and illustrations

Diagrams, charts, graphs and illustrations are visual representations of ideas. They can be used to support the text and communicate information.

## Diary

A diary is for writing about events and personal thoughts. It is like having a conversation with yourself. It is usually written daily and dated. No one should read anyone's diary without permission. There are also fictional diaries, eg an imaginary character writes a diary.

## Email (Electronic mail)

Email is messages and documents sent electronically through a computer via the Internet. Users can type messages to each other on the screen. Email messages usually consist of text, but images and documents can also be emailed (even animated images).

## Explanation text

Explanation text is writing that explains how something works or why it works. It is factual (true) writing and involves a sequence of events. It is usually in the present tense.

## Fax (Facsimile)

*Fax* is short for *facsimile*. A fax machine scans information from a page and sends it as a stream of signals along the telephone wire. A printer inside the receiving machine prints out the communication. Faxes are used to communicate quickly with people, for business or personal use. They should be clear and concise. They can be sent all around the world. The names and addresses of the sender and receiver are included on a fax.

## Genre

Genre means different kinds of writing. Some people call it 'text types'. There are different genres for fiction and nonfiction. Each genre has a certain kind of structure and grammar. Books often have more than one genre mixed within one text.

## Instructional text

Instructional texts (also called *procedural texts*) give instructions for others to read and follow. They follow a set procedure and have a definite form, for example recipes have a title, and are written under the headings *ingredients* and *method*.

## Invitation

An invitation is writing to ask a person to attend an event. Invitations should answer the questions *who, what, where* and *when*, give an RSVP date and return address. RSVP stands for the French *Respondez s'il vous plaît* — 'Reply if you please.'

## Journal

A journal contains reflective writing, which is recorded for a special purpose. People record observations, ideas and events in their journals. Personal, shortened language can be used. A journal is usually dated at the beginning of each entry.

## Journalism

Journalism is writing that is published in the media (newspapers, magazines etc). Journalism can be in the form of different genre such as reports, recounts or arguments (also called *expositions*).

## Letter

A letter (also called *correspondence*) is a form of writing to communicate with people. Letters can be used for personal or business communication. There are many different kinds of letters within these two groups. Letters usually follow a format — business letters need the address of the person writing, title and address of the person receiving the letter, greeting, body and a close. Personal letters usually just have a greeting, body and closing.

Letters can be formal or informal. Business letters are usually more formal; personal letters are usually more informal.

## List

A list is a clear, brief piece of writing to remind ourselves or others of simple bits of information. Each item begins a new line.

## Messages and memos

Messages and memos (short for *memoranda*) are short notes passed around in an informal way. People often use email to send messages and memos.

## Murder mystery

See *Crime fiction*.

## Narrative

A narrative is writing that tells a story. There are many different kinds of narrative including science fiction, horror, mystery, adventure and fantasy. Fiction narrative usually has an introduction that answers *when, where* and *who*, a complication or problem, and a resolution or ending of the problem. There are also narrative poems and factual narratives.

## Newspaper report

A newspaper report is writing for a newspaper. (See also *Journalism*.) Newspaper reports need snappy headlines, and a lead or introduction which answers *who, what, when* and *where* in the first paragraph. A newspaper report uses an inverted pyramid style of writing. This means the most important information is presented first — answers to the questions where, when, what and who — followed by less important details.

## Note taking

Note taking is a useful skill for keeping a brief record of anything. It is best to use key words or phrases to indicate the main points. Good note taking pays off. It is good for collecting ideas and bits of overheard conversation for writing stories.

## Novel

A novel is a very long story. Longer stories are often planned with chapters.

## Poetry

Poetry is writing in the form of verse. Poems can be any shape, size or form and be about any topic you choose. A poem does not have to rhyme, but it usually does have sound patterns or rhythm. Some poetry can follow a strict and regular rhythmic pattern. A poem can express thoughts and feelings of the writer, or it can be a narrative and tell a story. Poetry usually has a lot of imagery — word pictures created with metaphors, similes and personification.

## Procedural text

A procedural text is writing that tells how to do something through a sequence of actions or steps. Procedural texts are often called 'how-to' texts or instructional texts. See also *Instructional text*.

## Recount text

A recount text is writing that tells of past experiences. It is arranged in the sequence of time the events happened. It can be personal, factual or imaginary. It has a beginning that should answer who, when and where, a middle that is a series of sequenced events and an ending. The ending can include personal opinions, comments and findings. Journalists often write recounts in newspapers.

## Report

A report is writing that classifies and describes a topic. People write reports to organise and record factual information on a topic. Reports can classify and describe almost anything, for example, bikes, telephones, mountains or trees.

## Sentence

A sentence is a group of words that has a subject and a complete verb. It begins with a capital letter and ends with a full stop, exclamation mark or question mark.

## Traditional tales

Traditional tales are narratives. They began as oral stories told in countries all over the world and have been handed down over the years. They usually have a theme or message in them. Sometimes they are fairy tales that begin *Once upon a time.* Fables, fairy tales, folk tales, myths and legends are also traditional narratives.

## *Extra acknowledgment*

I am eternally grateful to my mum and Imogen Brunetti, secretary of the English Teachers' Association, for their help in writing the glossary.
x
**Cherry C**

# Index

acrostic poems 46
adjectives 23
advertisements 21, 58
alphabetical order 23, 49
animal narrative 30
arguments 59
atmosphere 10

ballad 58
business letters 60

case studies 23
cause and effect 15, 23
chapters 60
characters 5, 10, 11, 30
charts 16, 23, 24, 58
chronological order 26
classification 22, 23
classified advertising 21, 58
clues 10, 11, 58
commands 39
comparison 22, 23
correspondence 60
crime fiction 10, 11, 33, 58

description 22, 23
detective fiction (See 'crime fiction'.)
diagrams 15, 16, 23-24, 58
diary 58
display advertising 16, 21, 23, 24

electronic mail 58
email 40, 41, 58
epitaph 46
explanation text 14-16, 58
exposition 59

fables 30, 61
facsimile 20, 59
factual narrative 60
fairy tales 30, 61
fax (see facsimile)
fictional diary 58
fictional narrative 60
first person (I, we) 26
folk tales 30, 31, 60
fonts 40
frameworks 11, 15, 23, 27, 39, 57

genre 6, 59
graphs 16, 58

historical fiction 30
horror narrative 30
'how-to' texts (see procedural text)
humorous narrative 30

illustrations 16, 24, 58
imagery 61
instructional text (see procedural text)
interviews 36
inverted pyramid writing 57
invitation 42, 59

journal 59
journal entries 5
journalism 59

labels 16, 24
legends 30, 61
letter 60
linking words 22

lists 39, 43, 60

memos 48-49, 60
messages 15, 20, 35, 41, 42, 48-49, 60
metaphor 61
modern realistic narrative 30
murder mysteries (See 'crime fiction'.)
myths 30, 61

narrative 30, 31, 58, 60
narrative poems 58, 60, 61
newspaper recount 56, 61
newspaper report 36, 60
note-taking 60
notices 48-49
novel 60

opening statement 14, 15
opinions 27
orientation 30

paragraphs 36, 56
past tense 27, 57
personal letters 60
personal pronouns 27
persuasive writing 21, 58
planning 10, 23
plot 11
poetry 46-47, 54-55, 58, 61
pourquoi tales 30
present tense 15
procedural text 38, 39, 59, 61
pronouns 26

question and answer 23
questions 36

quotations 36

recipe 38
recount text 26, 27, 56, 59, 61
red herrings 10, 58
report 22, 23, 59, 60, 61
rhyme 47, 60
rhythm 60
RSVP 59

science fiction 30, 60
sentence 39, 61
setting 10, 30
shape poem 46
simile 16, 61
stanzas 58
summary 23, 27
suspects 11
suspense fiction (See 'crime fiction'.)

tense 15, 27, 57
theme 47
third person 57
traditional tales 30-31, 61

verbs 15, 22, 27
verse 61
visual thinking 23
visual representations 16, 23, 24, 58

whodunits (See 'crime fiction'.)